WORKBOOK

FOR

The Josiah Manifesto

(A Practical Guide to Jonathan Cahn's Book)

The Ancient Mystery & Guide for the End Times

Table of Content

Jonathan Cahn is the author of the book "The Josiah Manifesto: The Ancient Mystery and Guide for the End Times." This book delves into a combination of historical and biblical themes, providing a unique perspective on contemporary events and the potential significance of ancient prophecies in the context of the modern world. "The Josiah Manifesto: The Ancient Mystery & Guide for the End Times" can be purchased on Amazon.com. Within the scope of this conversation, we will analyze not less than a thousand words' worth of the book's most important ideas, themes, and consequences.

Jonathan Cahn, who is well-known for his prior writings such as "The Harbinger" and "The Paradigm," has gained notice for his ability to correlate biblical stories with events that are taking place in the present day. This legacy is continued in "The Josiah Manifesto," which, in addition to offering direction for navigating the intricacies of the end times, seeks to unearth the hidden secrets embedded within the historical and scriptural circumstances in which they occurred.

The figure of King Josiah, who plays a significant role in the Old Testament, particularly in the books of 2 Kings and 2 Chronicles, is at the center of "The Josiah Manifesto." During the reign of King Josiah, the Kingdom of Judah fell into a period of moral and spiritual degradation as well as increased idolatry. However, he was the one who began a religious renaissance by rediscovering the Book of the Law (possibly a reference to the Torah) within the temple, and then led his people back to worshiping the one and only true God. The comparison between Josiah's period and our own modern society, which is marked by moral uncertainty, societal turmoil, and spiritual detachment, serves as the basis for Cahn's investigation.

The following are some of the book's primary themes:

Rediscovering Ancient Knowledge: One of the most important ideas presented in "The Josiah Manifesto" is the concept that biblical narratives contain hidden ancient truths that continue to have significance in modern times. Cahn contends that we can gain significant insights that shed light on our present situations if we investigate the lives of biblical individuals and the happenings of their eras by looking at the historical context in which they lived.

The Last Days and Biblical Prophecy: Cahn says that the world is currently through what many people understand as the "end times"; this is a period of instability and uncertainty that was prophesied in a variety of religious sources, including the Bible. It is his contention that the deeds of biblical heroes such as Josiah might be utilized as pointers for navigating the challenges posed by the current era.

Revival of Spirituality: Cahn urges for a spiritual reawakening to take place in the current day in the same way that King Josiah's rediscovery of the Book of the Law resulted in a revival among the people of his kingdom. He encourages readers to rediscover their spiritual roots, look for greater truths, and develop a closer relationship with God by urging them to do all three.

The use of Symbols and Patterns: Cahn frequently makes use of the idea of patterns and symbols when attempting to draw links between historical events and incidents that are taking place today. He contends that there are certain patterns that recur throughout history and that these patterns serve as markers of higher spiritual truths.

Cultural Commentary: A critique of the values, moral decline, and disconnection from spiritual concepts that are prevalent in modern culture can be found in this book. Cahn contends that we may improve our decision-making in the here and now by reflecting on and learning from the errors of the past.

Individual Accountability: Cahn places a strong emphasis on the role that individuals play in bringing about constructive change. Readers are encouraged to accept personal responsibility for their deeds, beliefs, and the contributions they make to society in his writing.

The Current Significance of the Past: Cahn examines the concept that the past is not simply a collection of stories that have no bearing on the present, but rather that it contains vital lessons and knowledge that can direct our behavior in the here and now by using the story of Josiah as a lens.

It is necessary, when examining the ramifications of "The Josiah Manifesto," to appreciate both the positive aspects and the negative aspects of Cahn's approach. His ability to create links between historical and biblical accounts and modern occurrences is one of their strengths. This has the potential to provide readers a new feeling of perspective as well as a refreshed comprehension of their role within the greater narrative of human history. In addition, people who are looking for more profound meaning in a society that moves quickly and is frequently shallow may find that Cahn's appeal for spiritual renewal and human responsibility strikes a chord with them.

On the other hand, there have been some voiced objections. Cahn's readings of historical events and biblical texts, according to the arguments of certain academics, may be subjective and speculative, which could lead to potential misunderstandings of the text. In addition, he has a propensity to draw analogies between historical occurrences and contemporary circumstances, which may result in an oversimplification of complicated topics and a failure to recognize the complexities that form contemporary concerns. Some critics doubt the validity of drawing direct analogies between the deeds of a historical character like Josiah and the intricacies of today's global concerns. Josiah was a biblical king who lived in the 10th century B.C.E. and is mentioned in the Bible.

In conclusion, "The Josiah Manifesto: The Ancient Mystery and Guide for the End Times" by Jonathan Cahn tries to investigate the importance of historical and biblical narratives in comprehending and navigating the challenges of the modern world. Cahn's book is subtitled "The Ancient Mystery and Guide for the End Times." Cahn draws similarities to today's moral degradation by focusing on King Josiah's revival during a time of spiritual decline. He then advocates for a revival of faith, individual responsibility, and a greater connection to eternal truths. King Josiah was able to turn things around during a time when spirituality was in decline. The book offers a perspective that is thought-provoking and encourages reflection; nonetheless, readers should approach the book's ideas with a critical eye and evaluate its interpretations in the context of wider historical and theological knowledge.

Certain occurrences in the ever-shifting panorama of human history appear to be directed by forces that go beyond the randomness of chance. In his book "The Josiah Manifesto: The Ancient Mystery and Guide for the End Times," author Jonathan Cahn dives into the intriguing thought that a three-thousand-year old calendar may contain the key to comprehending some of the most dramatic events in our lives. Cahn believes that the Josiah calendar may have been used to predict the end of the world as we know it. The assertions stated in the book will be investigated in this workbook, with a particular emphasis placed on the appointed days, predictions, and the significant impact of this ancient calendar.

1. The Importance of Appointed Days

Chapter 2 of Jonathan Cahn's book "The Josiah Manifesto: The Ancient Mystery and Guide for the End Times" looks into the intriguing subject of the significance of assigned days throughout history. Cahn's book is titled "The Ancient Mystery and Guide for the End Times." Cahn proposes the theory that some defining events in history have been foreordained and designated by a higher power, and that these periods line up with the feasts described in the Bible and the patterns described in prophecy. This topic will be covered in greater depth in the following section of the workbook. Readers will be prompted to analyze the impact that designated days have had on the course of human history.

- **Comprehending the Concept of Appointed Days**

Cahn presents the idea that appointed days are not coincidental occurrences but rather are events that were purposefully woven into the fabric of time. Drawing on ancient literature and historical narratives, he proposes that these set days are endowed with profound spiritual value, and that they frequently represent the intents or prophesies of supernatural beings. Cahn's argument that there may be a larger cosmic design at work is based on the fact that he has aligned these days with key historical events.

- **Discussion and Reflection on the Past:**

The reader is encouraged to give some thought to the concept of designated days as well as the significance they have. The author invites the reader to reflect on times in their own lives or in history that were exceptionally fated or significant to them. Readers can evaluate whether or not these moments could possibly correspond with the concept of appointed days through serious debate.

- **Exploring Biblical and Historical Patterns**

Cahn suggests that there is a relationship between ancient rites and contemporary occurrences by drawing parallels between the biblical feasts and appointed days throughout history. For instance, the Feast of Passover is connected to the idea of deliverance, and Cahn gives examples from history of notable deliverances that took place on or around the time of Passover. This pattern is not restricted to a single festival, but rather it incorporates a variety of biblical observances.

- **Workbook Activity**

The readers are given an exercise in the accompanying workbook that allows them to explore deeper into the idea. Readers are urged to do their own study and come up with examples of times in which historical events coincided with biblical feasts or other noteworthy dates. The purpose of this exercise is to encourage readers to become actively involved with historical accounts and critically evaluate whether or not certain alignments could in fact be indicative of appointed days.

- **Symbolism Interpretation**

In this chapter, Cahn goes into further detail regarding the symbolism that is connected to specific designated days. He says that these days frequently hold significant prophetic and spiritual connotations that are reflected in the events that are unfolding at this time. The reader is prompted in the workbook to interpret the symbolism linked with particular designated days and ponder how it might relate to historical events.

- **Considering Divine Intervention**

The belief that certain occurrences are predetermined by a higher power or supernatural intervention can be brought up in conversation when discussing the concept of appointed days. The reader is encouraged to investigate their own ideas regarding fate, destiny, and the involvement of divine intervention in human affairs through the use of the workbook. This introspection encourages readers to wrestle with some of the more difficult problems concerning free will and destiny.

- **Relevance to the Events of the Present**

The reader is encouraged to apply their newfound understanding of appointed days to current events as they continue to explore the concept of appointed days presented in the workbook. Readers are able to determine whether or not any noteworthy occurrences coincide with the concept of appointed days by conducting an examination of previous historical situations. An increased awareness of the ways in which history and spirituality are intertwined can be cultivated via the use of this application.

Conclusion: This chapter of the workbook comes to a close by putting an emphasis on the concept that appointed days are not simply remnants of the past but rather continue to play a role in the process of forming our comprehension of history and spirituality. Readers are encouraged to investigate the complex interrelationships that exist between the divine, human action, and the progression of pivotal events by musing over the meaning of specific points in the narrative.

As readers progress through this chapter, they will develop a more nuanced understanding of the concept of appointed days and the ways in which these days may affect the development of historical events. This examination lays the groundwork for future investigation into the prophesies and interpretations that are offered in later chapters of "The Josiah Manifesto," allowing readers to evaluate the potential ramifications of these concepts on both their worldview and their comprehension of the world around them.

2. The Unveiling of Prophecies

The disclosure of predictions that had been concealed inside the framework of the old calendar. This chapter dives into particular examples of prophesies that are supposed to have dramatically unfolded in modern times. Some of the events that are discussed in this chapter include a pandemic, a national lockdown, days of fire, and the changing of the Supreme Court. This workbook delves into these examples in great detail, challenging readers to conduct an in-depth analysis of the information that Cahn has offered.

- **Prophecies: From the Ancient Calendar to Current Events**

Cahn presents the theory that the ancient calendar contains encoded predictions that transcend millennia and have a substantial impact on important events throughout the history of humanity. The reader is led through an understanding of the structure of these predictions by the workbook, which places an emphasis on the deep connection that exists between the symbolism of the calendar and the events that it is claimed to predict.

Case Study 1: *The Prophecy of the Plague and the National Lockdown*

Cahn uncovers the claimed prophecy that is connected to a plague and a national lockdown in this section of the book. He describes the historical occurrences that correspond with this prophecy and emphasizes the symbolic importance of these occurrences with regard to the calendar. The reader is prompted throughout the workbook to evaluate the material that was provided by Cahn, making comparisons with historical data and different potential explanations.

Case Study 2: *The Days of Fire and the Transformation of the Supreme Court*

The "days of fire" concept as well as the evolution of the Supreme Court are the topics that are covered in the next section of the workbook. According to Cahn, these predictions are intimately intertwined into the fabric of history, and as a result, they shape the path that nations take. The reader is challenged to research the historical occurrences that are associated with these prophesies and to consider whether the linkages that are offered have any basis in reality.

- **Evaluating the Relationships**

The reader is encouraged to take a more critical stance throughout this section of the workbook. The reader is asked to analyze the validity of the connections between the predictions and the happenings, taking into consideration elements such as the historical context, the causation, and alternate explanations. The examination of the allegations that Cahn has made can benefit from a more even-handed approach thanks to this exercise.

- **The Part That Interpretation Plays**

Cahn places a strong emphasis on the importance of interpretation when it comes to deciphering prophesies. The workbook encourages readers to engage in conversations regarding the subjectivity of interpretation and the possibility that different people may arrive at different conclusions based on the same data. Readers are given the ability to have a more in-depth engagement with the subject matter when the intricacies of interpretation are acknowledged.

- **Exploring the Opposing Arguments**

The prophecies that are revealed in the book are challenged by other viewpoints in the accompanying workbook, which aims to give an all-encompassing viewpoint. The reader is urged to conduct a critical analysis of these counterarguments, consider the evidence on both sides and come to a well-informed decision regarding the validity of the linkages that Cahn has given.

- **Introspection Regarding One's Own Beliefs**

At the end of the chapter, the author encourages readers to give some thought to their own perspectives on divine intervention in history, prophecy, and historical causation. Readers are urged to engage in self-reflection and evaluate the degree to which their preexisting views coincide with or diverge from those outlined in the text of the book. This reflection encourages one to have a more profound comprehension of their own perspective.

- **Conversation in addition to the Group Activity**

The reader is able to engage in dialogues with other individuals who have also read the book because the companion workbook contains a discussion and group activity component. This feature of interactivity encourages deliberate exchanges of ideas, giving readers the opportunity to gain knowledge from a variety of viewpoints and investigate a range of possible interpretations of the subject matter.

Conclusion: *Navigating Prophecy and History*
The final point that this chapter of the workbook makes is to emphasize how difficult it can be to decipher predictions and how closely they relate to past occurrences. When interacting with the information that is provided in "The Josiah Manifesto," readers are asked to

keep an open mind, critically assess the evidence supplied, and proceed with their investigation into the junction between prophecy, historical events, and spirituality.

The reader lays the groundwork for the subsequent chapters by deeply engaging with the claims stated in this chapter. In the next chapters, the reader will dive further into the mysteries of the ancient calendar and its potential implications for understanding the unfolding of key events in our world.

3. Skepticism and Alternative Explanations

This chapter acknowledges the natural tendency to question remarkable claims and invites readers to critically assess the assertions made throughout the book. This chapter also acknowledges the inherent tendency to question extraordinary claims. This workbook dives into the function of skepticism in intellectual research and investigates several alternative viewpoints that may present a challenge to the interpretations that have been given.

- **Taking a Skeptical Attitude**

At the beginning of the chapter, there is a recognition of the importance of skepticism in any intellectual endeavor. This highlights the fact that skepticism is not intended to be an absolute rejection of ideas but rather to expose them to thorough investigation instead. The reader is encouraged to develop a mindset that is skeptical while interacting with the arguments that are presented in the book by following the instructions in the accompanying workbook.

- **The Significance of Analytical and Critical Thinking**

When evaluating the assertions stated in "The Josiah Manifesto," readers are encouraged to apply the critical thinking skills taught in the accompanying workbook. It offers a structure for analyzing evidence, locating logical fallacies, and determining whether or not arguments are coherent. The reader is asked to evaluate the quality of the evidence as well as the soundness of the thinking that lies behind the various prophesies that are presented in the book.

- **Taking into account the effect of confirmation bias**

The assertions made by Cahn may ring true for readers who hold analogous values or perspectives on the world. The concept of confirmation bias is brought to light in the accompanying workbook. This prejudice refers to the tendency of individuals to favor information that confirms their preexisting beliefs. The reader is invited to consider their own possible prejudices and how such biases might have an effect on how they understand the material they are reading.

- **Exploring Potentially Competing Explanations**

In this part of the workbook, readers are prompted to think about other possible explanations for the events and patterns that were covered in the main text of the book. This includes taking into consideration historical, sociopolitical, and cultural aspects of the world that may have played a role in the occurrences. Readers get a more comprehensive comprehension of the complexities of historical causation when they engage with several perspectives throughout the reading experience.

- **Interactive Activity: Interpretation Debate**

The reader participates in a debate-style discussion on the interpretations offered in the book through an activity that is included in the workbook as an interactive activity. This game invites readers to assume a variety of positions, either defending or questioning the arguments that Cahn has stated. This activity helps to cultivate a mindset of rational skepticism as well as discussion that is courteous.

- **Engaging with the Opinions of Experts**

The chapter encourages readers to explore the perspectives of specialists in a variety of subjects, including history, theology, and archaeology, among others. Having in-depth conversations with industry professionals might yield insightful takeaways and new points of view on the subjects covered in the book. The workbook provides suggestions for getting access to credible sources and participating in informed conversations.

- **Taking a Look at Some Erroneous Interpretations and Statements**

There is no piece of work that is safe from mistakes or misunderstandings. The reader is encouraged to be vigilant in searching for any possible errors or misunderstandings in the claims that Cahn has made by using the worksheet. Through participation in this activity, readers are prompted to interact with the content on a more profound level and to subject the claims to a higher level of examination.

- **Finding a Happy Medium Between Openness and Skepticism**

The chapter comes to a close by emphasizing how critical it is to maintain an open mind while maintaining a healthy dose of healthy skepticism. Skepticism is a useful tool for keeping critical thought alive, but it is equally important to keep an open mind to new ideas and points of view. The reader is prompted throughout the workbook to approach the subject matter with an attitude of curiosity and a willingness to explore beyond their established boundaries of safety and security.

Conclusion: Navigating the Inquiry Journey

This chapter of the workbook places an emphasis on the idea that skepticism is not a goal but rather an essential step along the path of intellectual inquiry. Readers can improve their knowledge of the content of the book as well as the consequences of that information by engaging critically with the material and taking into consideration several alternative explanations. The more the readers investigate, the more prepared they are to make educated judgments on the statements presented in "The Josiah Manifesto" and its significance in their own lives.

When it comes to the historical occurrences that have played a role in the formation of nations and cultures, there are very few that are as mysterious and influential as the incident that occurred on Capitol Hill and sent shockwaves across the country. As recommended by Jonathan Cahn in his thought-provoking work "The Josiah Manifesto: The Ancient Mystery & Guide for the End Times," in order to appreciate the multifarious character of this event, one must delve into the interplay of several factors. This is a suggestion that was made by Jonathan Cahn. Within the confines of this framework, the confluence of an ancient temple, an ominous prayer, and a mystery template reveals a complex network of symbolism, historical echoes, and prophetic overtones that may offer light on the turmoil on Capitol Hill.

1. The Obscene Prayer: A Portal to Powers That Cannot Be Seen

It has been known for a long time that prayer is a channel through which humans can connect with the divine. It is also a way for people to express their wishes, appreciation, and requests for direction. Nevertheless, Jonathan Cahn's investigation of a sinister prayer presents a thought that is both provocative and disconcerting in the context of the field of spiritual communication. Cahn digs on the idea that prayers can bear unintended consequences and become portals to unseen forces that influence the course of history in his book titled "The Josiah Manifesto: The Ancient Mystery & Guide for the End Times." It is vital to deconstruct the many layers of an ominous prayer and how it may intertwine with the incident that transpired on Capitol Hill in order to fully grasp the relevance of this idea. This will allow one to see how the two may be related.

- **Unveiling the Unintended: The Power of Intent**

Intentions that go deeper than the surface level can be contained inside prayers, which are typically understood to be requests for favors. The realization that the intentions behind a prayer can have rippling effects that extend far beyond the immediate supplicant is at the heart of Cahn's investigation of the sinister prayer. In the same way that having positive intentions can lead to beneficial results, having negative intentions might accidentally release forces that were not intended. In the context of the upheaval on Capitol Hill, the idea of an ominous prayer prompts one to ponder whether the event was triggered by motives that were covert, divisive, or even evil. This line of inquiry is prompted by the fact that the concept of an ominous prayer promotes thought. Because of this, the focus is moved from the physical activities to the metaphysical realm of intention, and as a result, it is a significant aspect in interpreting the event's broader significance.

- **A Catalyst for Unseen Forces: The Meeting of Intent and Reality**

Cahn's exploration of the sinister prayer reveals a dimension of causality that is not limited to the physical realm. It indicates that when intentions are aligned with historical circumstances, significant forces can be invoked that influence results. The event that took place on Capitol Hill could be understood as a convergence of intents and realities, or a junction where the ephemeral power of prayer and intention meets the material world of action and effect. This is one possible interpretation of what took place. This concept resonates with the idea that historical events are shaped by a complex interaction of visible and unseen variables, where human acts and the forces they summon become entwined in ways that challenge conventional comprehension. In other words, the idea that historical events are molded by a complex interplay of visible and invisible factors is supported by this concept.

- **The Echoes of Destiny: Prophecy and Precedent**

Cahn's investigation of the ominous prayer focuses mostly on the prayer's resonance with the prophetic. This is one of the most important aspects of this investigation. It is common for prophecy to imply foreknowledge of future events, suggesting that there is a set course that future occurrences are destined to follow. The idea that particular prayers, especially those that are loaded with evil intentions, might act as catalysts for momentous events is consistent with the concept of destiny as the unfolding of a series of events that are intertwined with one another. The upheaval on Capitol Hill, when viewed in this light, becomes the fulfillment of a prearranged narrative. It is also a manifestation of the echoes of history, and it serves as a reminder that the interplay between intention, action, and prophesy is more complex than it initially appears.

Conclusion: Illuminating the Unseen Forces

The idea that an ominous prayer can act as a gateway to unseen powers was proposed by Jonathan Cahn. This idea serves as a powerful invitation to investigate the complex forces that have shaped the course of human history. It calls into question the conventional ideas of causality and encourages a more in-depth investigation into the motivations and energy that lie behind noteworthy occurrences. When applied to the event that took place on Capitol Hill, this notion inspires an investigation into the possible hidden motivations, ideological clashes, and cosmic resonances that contributed to the upheaval. This study could lead to the discovery of a hidden motive, ideological clash, or cosmic resonance. The investigation of the ominous prayer opens doors to comprehending the hidden elements of history as well as the intricate interplay between purpose and effect. This is true regardless of whether the investigation is taken as a cautionary tale or as a revelation of the mysterious forces at play.

2. Unlocking the Secrets of the Blueprint: The Mysterious Template

Certain incidents in the historical tapestry stand out as more than mere coincidences; they appear to follow a highly organized sequence, like parts of a grand design coming together. These occurrences seem to follow a carefully orchestrated sequence, like they are following a deliberately orchestrated sequence. Jonathan Cahn's investigation of a mystery template in "The Josiah Manifesto: The Ancient Mystery & Guide for the End Times" provides an intriguing concept that compels us to contemplate the presence of a complex blueprint behind key occurrences. Cahn's book is titled "The Josiah Manifesto: The Ancient Mystery & Guide for the End Times." This idea encourages us to decipher the underlying structure that may have been responsible for directing the path that history took within the context of the event that took place on Capitol Hill.

- **The Construction of Meaning Based on Historical Blueprints**

The use of a blueprint to serve as a fundamental plan and direct the building of a complicated structure is common practice. When applied to historical occurrences, the concept of a mystery template hints at the existence of a predetermined chain of events or conditions that shaped the final result. This investigation by Cahn invites us to consider history not only as a collection of haphazardly occurring events, but rather as a purposeful composition that is directed by forces that are beyond our immediate grasp. When we look at the chaotic event that occurred on Capitol Hill through this lens, we are tempted to question whether or not covert variables and historical echoes coincided according to a disguised design, possibly driven by deeper cosmic or spiritual forces. When we do this, we are drawn to believe that deeper cosmic or spiritual forces were at work.

- **The Importance of Synchrony in the Alignment of Threads**

Synchronicity is defined as the happening of seemingly unrelated occurrences that coincide in a meaningful manner. Cahn's idea of a mystery template compels us to investigate synchronicity. The upheaval on Capitol Hill may be considered as the culmination of a series of threads that combined to produce a dramatic story. There were a variety of factors that came together to form this narrative. This interaction of aspects, whether political, social, or even metaphysical, could be perceived as being orchestrated by a bigger plan. This could be the case whether the interplay is political, social, or even metaphysical. In the same way that a template provides the coherence of an artistic creation, the mysterious template may imply that historical events, despite having multiple facets, follow a general pattern that determines the way in which they unfold.

- **The Cosmic Blueprint: Revelations from the Ancient Past**

The importance that Cahn places on the end of times brings into sharper relief the idea of a cosmic blueprint. In the context of prophecy, historical events are frequently viewed as stages on the way to a predetermined climax. The notion that a secret template is at work behind the scenes on Capitol Hill is congruent with the concept of events on the hill serving to fulfill a larger narrative. This raises intriguing questions about whether the upheaval, while rooted in individual circumstances, is also part of a cosmic plan — a succession of occurrences that repeat prophetic insights, contributing to the unfolding of a larger script that transcends the immediate moment. These concerns are raised because this raises intriguing questions about whether the upheaval is also founded in specific conditions.

Conclusion: Revealing the Unseen Order

Our comprehension of causality and interconnection receives a huge boost in both breadth and depth when we apply it to the investigation of a mystery template set against the backdrop of key historical events. The insights provided by Jonathan Cahn invite us to move beyond a linear perspective on history and to embrace the idea that events may evolve according to a hidden order. By decoding the design that underlay the event that took place on Capitol Hill, we are given the opportunity to investigate the confluence of intentions, conditions, and influences that may have been organized by forces that transcend beyond the confines of the visible world. When we consider the idea of a mysterious template, we are inspired to realize that the complicated dance that is history is led by threads of meaning and intention, which weave together to form the vast tapestry that is the human experience.

3. Interweaving the Threads: Unveiling Interpretations

In the rich tapestry that is human history, the unfolding of events frequently leaves us with more questions than answers. The occurrence that took place on Capitol Hill and rattled the entire country is not an exception to this rule. In the thought-provoking book titled "The Josiah Manifesto: The Ancient Mystery & Guide for the End Times," written by Jonathan Cahn, the interaction of an old temple, a foreboding prayer, and a cryptic template provides a prism through which we might attempt to decipher the complexities of this significant incident. This allows us to better understand the significance of this event. We might be able to unearth previously unknown meanings, historical echoes, and significant insights on the event's significance if we interweave these strands.

- **The Symbolism and the Power of the Ancient Temple**

Ancient temples have, for a very long time, been recognized as symbols of religious devotion and cultural import. We recognize a striking contrast by drawing analogies to Capitol Hill, which serves as the nerve center of American government. Capitol Hill has a function analogous to that of ancient temples when it comes to the concentration of power and devotion in their respective communities. When viewed as a confluence of symbolic power, the event's impact takes on greater significance; it is as if the distant past is resonating in the here and now, serving as a reminder that historical forces continue to influence the course that nations take.

Intentions and Unseen Forces, as Revealed by the Ominous Prayer

The exploration that Cahn performs on the ominous prayer presents a concept that is both puzzling and thought-provoking. Prayers, which are often thought of as a way to communicate with the supernatural, might contain intentions that lead to outcomes that are unexpected. The idea that a sinister prayer can open a door to unseen powers hints at a significant interaction between the spiritual and the material realms. When considered in the context of the upheaval on Capitol Hill, this idea throws open doors to comprehending the underlying currents of intention, the convergence of desires, and the possible impact of metaphysical forces on historical events.

- **The Mysterious Model: Directing the Progress of the Unfolding**

A cryptic framework suggests that there is an overarching plan directing the progression of the events. It chimes with the concept that historical events develop in accordance with a complex blueprint, which is a concept that is not unfamiliar to prophetic and cosmic interpretations. When viewed through the lens of a template, the event that took place on Capitol Hill sheds light on the interconnectivity of acts and intents. When seemingly unrelated events come together, they become a part of a larger story, resembling a cosmic symphony in which each note plays an important part in the overall composition.

- **Conceptual Integration: A Look at the Bigger Picture**

The way in which these ideas are intertwined results in the formation of a narrative that goes beyond the confines of traditional analysis. The old temple serves as a setting, the foreboding prayer acts as a driving force, and the mystery blueprint is a compass for what follows next. They work together to reveal a tapestry that is woven from the intersection of intention, symbolism, and fate. When viewed through this prism, the upheaval on Capitol Hill is not only the result of a single occurrence but rather a reflection of the delicate dance that occurs between humans, the holy, and the cosmos.

Conclusion: Uncovering Meaningful Layers

When one investigates the intersection of a long-ago temple, a foreboding prayer, and a puzzling pattern, hidden dimensions are brought into view, which is helpful when one is trying to comprehend something that occurred on a grand scale. The insights provided by Cahn encourage us to understand history as a multi-dimensional canvas that has layers of symbolism, intention, and supernatural intervention painted upon it. Exploration of these threads reveals that significant events are never isolated moments but rather integral parts of a larger narrative — a narrative that stretches back into time and extends forward into the mysterious realm of the future. This is true whether these threads are viewed through the lens of spirituality, prophecy, or historical resonance.

1. The enigmatic Ancient King

The motif of the mysterious long-dead king appears again and again in a wide variety of historical texts, religious writings, and literary works. These historical characters are frequently presented as individuals possessing a tremendous deal of knowledge, mystique, and significance, whose deeds and teachings continue to have value well beyond their own time period. This archetype has captivated the imaginations of people from all different cultures and time periods, and it is frequently employed as a method in storytelling to communicate profound truths and insights. In "The Josiah Manifesto: The Ancient Mystery & Guide for the End Times" by Jonathan Cahn, the mysterious ancient ruler certainly plays a vital role in imparting secret wisdom that has contemporary application. Cahn's book is titled

"The Josiah Manifesto: The Ancient Mystery &
Guide for the End Times."

The Enigmatic Ancient King's Attributes:

Knowledge: The mysterious ancient king is
often shown as having remarkable wisdom and
insight into the world around him. Their
judgments and the lessons they taught are seen
as sources of direction that extend beyond the
time period in which they occurred. In the case
of "The Josiah Manifesto," this insight may have
its origins in spiritual and moral concepts that
are still applicable to readers living in the
present world.

Mystery: The word "enigmatic" suggests that
there is some aspect of secretiveness and allure
surrounding the figure. It's possible that their
deeds or their lessons are veiled in symbols, and
in order to decipher them, you'll need to give
great consideration to how to understand them.
The reader is encouraged to dive more into the
meaning of the text by the presence of this

enigma, which provides the narrative with additional depth.

Historical Influence: The deeds of the mysterious ancient king frequently had long-lasting repercussions for the culture or nation that he ruled. Because of their ability to bring about positive change through their leadership, reforms, or spiritual insights, they may become revered individuals in history. This historical influence can be compared to the concept of a modern president of the United States overcoming obstacles and leaving a legacy.

Spiritual and moral guidance: The mysterious ancient king's cryptic teachings frequently focus on ethical and spiritual precepts as their primary themes. These lessons have the potential to act as a compass for individuals or leaders who are confronted with difficult decisions, ethical conundrums, or societal issues. The puzzling teachings of an ancient king are presented in "The Josiah Manifesto," which may serve as a moral compass for the president of the United States today.

The relevance of this to "The Josiah Manifesto" is as follows:

In the book written by Jonathan Cahn, the mysterious ancient king could act as a connection between the past and the present, providing insights that shed light on the spiritual and moral implications of the events that are occurring in the present day. It is possible that the legacy of the king contains the answers to concerns that contemporary society struggles to resolve, whether these questions are about leadership, justice, or righteousness, or if they concern the pursuit of a higher purpose.

There is a possibility that the role of the mysterious old monarch is connected in some way to the investigation of ancient mysteries and their relevance to the end of the world in this book. In the same way that historical individuals such as King Josiah negotiated key points in history, the current President of the

United States of America may encounter obstacles that are representative of a greater narrative relating to prophecy, spirituality, and the transformation of society.

Conclusion: The archetype of the mysterious old ruler is a potent storytelling device that is independent of both time and society. It is a captivating tool for delivering significant truths and insights because it encompasses wisdom, a sense of mystery, and the significance that history has bestowed upon it. In the context of "The Josiah Manifesto," this archetype most likely plays an important part in connecting ancient wisdom with modern issues, bringing insight and perspective to the contemporary narrative. This archetype may also play a role in connecting ancient wisdom with modern challenges. The reader can obtain a greater grasp of the book's topics and its message about utilizing timeless principles to manage the complexity of the end times and modern life by investigating the mysterious ancient king's teachings and activities.

2. The Modern American President

The depiction of a contemporary American president within "The Josiah Manifesto: The Ancient Mystery & Guide for the End Times" by Jonathan Cahn most likely serves as a symbolic representation of contemporary leadership, societal challenges, and the need for spiritual guidance in the midst of complex issues. Cahn wrote "The Josiah Manifesto: The Ancient Mystery & Guide for the End Times." This character exemplifies the challenges and responsibilities that are encountered by leaders in a society that is fast changing, and the trip that they take may mirror the themes and lessons that are presented in the book.

Attributes of the Modern American President:

Leadership problems It is possible that the modern President of the United States portrayed in this book is meant to reflect a leader who is attempting to overcome a variety of problems, including political, social, economic, and ethical issues. The complexity of modern governance is reflected in these issues, which may be analogous to the difficult circumstances that actual leaders must navigate in the real world.

Location at a National Crossroads: In the same way that King Josiah guided Judah through a critical time period, the modern president may steer the country at a crossroads in the nation's history. This could encompass challenges relating to shifts in culture, technical breakthroughs, global relations, and ideological conflicts; all of these things are reflective of the dynamic aspect of the contemporary world.

Ethical Conundrums: The journey of the president could contain difficult moral choices that put their morals and principles to the test. The decisions that individuals make could have an effect not only on their own personal legacy but also on the course that the country takes. This is a reflection of the ethical issues that leaders frequently encounter when trying to balance the interests of competing groups.

Spiritual Quest: In keeping with the overarching topic of the book, the path to becoming a modern president can involve a search for a more profound spiritual understanding and wisdom. This may involve searching for old teachings, truths, or insights that offer direction in navigating the intricacies of their role as a leader.

The relevance of this to "The Josiah Manifesto" is as follows:

The characterization of the current President of the United States in "The Josiah Manifesto" provides a potential entry point for delving deeper into the book's core ideas. It's possible that their contacts with the mysterious ancient king's teachings or revelations indicate the melding of historical wisdom with the challenges of the present day. It's possible that the president's receptivity to these lessons reflects a readiness to see beyond political and chronological limitations in the discovery of more profound truths.

The character journey of the president could also emphasize the significance of humility, introspection, and a willingness to gain knowledge from one's mistakes in the past. It's possible that their path will be similar to the overarching message of the book, which is that decoding old riddles and figuring out how to apply them to modern problems might lead to a deeper comprehension, a more meaningful life, and an alignment with spiritual realities.

Conclusion: It is possible that the depiction of a contemporary American president in "The Josiah Manifesto: The Ancient Mystery & Guide for the End Times" serves as a symbolic image of contemporary leadership and the issues that are encountered by leaders in a world that is continuously changing. The author has the opportunity to go into topics like as leadership, moral conundrums, and the quest for spiritual direction via the lens of this character. The interactions of the president with the teachings of the mysterious old king may highlight the need of incorporating ancient wisdom into modern decision-making processes, which will ultimately result in a deeper sense of purpose and harmony with spiritual truths. Through the utilization of this character archetype, the book has the potential to engage readers in a reflective investigation of the intricate dynamic that exists between history, prophecy, spirituality, and leadership.

3. Uncovering the Secret

In "The Josiah Manifesto: The Ancient Mystery & Guide for the End Times" by Jonathan Cahn, the idea of "unveiling the secret" most likely occupies a pivotal position in the story's progression. This concept encompasses the notion of unearthing previously concealed truths, insights, and pieces of knowledge from the past that have bearing on the here and now as well as the future. The revelation of the secret may mark a turning point in the narrative of the book, one in which the mysterious ancient king's teachings or deeds become clear and have an effect on the path traveled by the contemporary President of the United States.

Uncovering the Secret:

The Symbolism of Revelation: It's possible that the "secret" represents a more profound comprehension of spiritual truths, historical patterns, or prophetic insights. The discovery of these previously obscured links is brought to light as a result of its unfolding, which is a moment that symbolizes clarity and revelation.

Seeking Wisdom: It's possible that, during the course of the novel, the characters' journey to discover the secret is a reflection of humanity's innate urge to seek knowledge and comprehension. This inquiry could involve translating ancient manuscripts, figuring out the meanings of various symbols, and establishing connections between past events and modern problems.

Transformation of Consciousness: It is possible that the revelation of the secret will bring about a spiritual awakening for both the mysterious ancient ruler and the current President of the United States. This awakening may involve a profound realization of their responsibilities in the wider narrative of history and the necessity to align their acts with higher spiritual ideals.

This awakening may also involve a desire to align their actions with these principles.

The relevance of this to "The Josiah Manifesto" is as follows:

It's possible that the revelation of the secret will act as a defining moment in the story's progression. It is possible that this is the juncture at which the mysterious old king's teachings, deeds, or predictions are unearthed, so setting in motion a chain of events that determine the path that the current president of the United States of America takes in terms of his leadership and decision-making.

The basic idea of the book is to connect ancient knowledge with the concerns of the modern world, and this topic emphasizes that connection. The revelation of the secret might provide insights that help modern presidents better comprehend their obligations, the nation's purpose, and the larger context of the end times when it comes to which times they are living in.

Consequences & Repercussions: Providing Direction for Determination Purposes:

If the secret were to be revealed, it might give today's president a compass for navigating the difficult choices that face the country. It is possible that the president will make decisions that are in accordance with higher moral and spiritual values if he takes the mysterious old king's advice into consideration.

Leadership that brings about transformation: The revelation of the secret might encourage the sitting president of the United States of today to adopt a transformative style of leadership. They might make the well-being of the nation their top priority, pursue justice, foster togetherness, and solve societal difficulties in ways that are consonant with the teachings of the mysterious old monarch.

Inspiration and Guidance: If the secret were to be revealed, it might give the story a sense of direction and give the character's reason to hope. It could be interpreted to suggest that even in times of unpredictability and upheaval, there are eternal truths that can lead individuals, nations, and the world as a whole toward a bright and meaningful future.

Conclusion: The "unveiling of the secret" serves as an effective storytelling device that emphasizes the fundamental ideas presented in "The Josiah Manifesto." It is a symbol of the aha! moment that occurs when previously unknown knowledge from the past suddenly becomes a beacon of light for the present. The book investigates the transforming power of ancient teachings, the relevance of aligning one's behavior with spiritual principles, and the potential for positive change even in turbulent times through the lens of this concept. The revelation of the secret acts as a catalyst for the journey of the current president of the United States of America. It is a symbol of their ambition to lead with wisdom, purpose, and a profound grasp of the many threads that make up history.

4. Ancient Knowledge Applied to Today's World

Ancient Wisdom for Modern Times" is a major topic in many different spiritual, intellectual, and literary works, and it is possible that it carries significance in "The Josiah Manifesto: The Ancient Mystery & Guide for the End Times" by Jonathan Cahn. This topic places an emphasis on the ageless quality of knowledge as well as its relevance to issues that are prevalent in modern society. In the context of the book, it would involve the mysterious ancient king's teachings or acts providing advice and insight to the contemporary President of the United States as they negotiate difficult situations.

- **Exploring Ancient Wisdom for Today**

The concept of ancient knowledge underlines the idea that certain truths and principles are not confined by the restrictions of time. This idea is highlighted by the phrase "transcending time." Although they originated in the distant past, the teachings of the mysterious ancient king have a timeless quality that makes them applicable to individuals and leaders in any time period.

- **Moral and ethical guidance**

The moral and ethical lessons that should be carried forward from culture to culture and generation to generation are frequently included in ancient wisdom. These teachings have the potential to act as a moral compass for the president of the United States of America in the current era, assisting them in making judgments that are consistent with justice, compassion, and honesty.

- **Application in Practice**

Ancient wisdom is not simply a theoretical concept; it can be applied to circumstances that occur in the real world. It is possible that the deeds of the mysterious ancient king can provide examples of good leadership, conflict resolution, or spiritual practices that have direct significance for the issues faced by the modern president.

The relevance of this to "The Josiah Manifesto" is as follows:

It is likely that "The Josiah Manifesto" gives major consideration to the idea of applying timeless knowledge to contemporary problems. The teachings of the mysterious ancient king could provide a model for the current president of the United States to follow in order to handle contemporary challenges such as political polarization, social inequality, environmental concerns, and international wars. The president has the ability to strive toward the creation of a society that is more just, harmonious, and spiritually linked by adopting universally applicable ideals.

Consequences & Repercussions: Decision-Making Guidance The wisdom of the ancient king could offer the current president of the United States guidance in the area of decision-making that is both ethical and principled. This instruction may extend to issues pertaining to foreign policy, economic change, measures pertaining to social justice, and possibly even more.

Fostering Cohesion Through: The interdependence of all people is a theme that frequently appears in ancient texts. The implementation of these lessons by the president has the potential to foster unity and cooperation, urging individuals to put aside their differences and work together for the benefit of society as a whole.

Transformation of the Individual: It's possible that the president will experience personal growth and change as a result of his interaction with ancient knowledge. They could have a more profound comprehension of the position that they play as a leader as well as the obligation that comes with it to defend spiritual and moral standards.

Conclusion: The theme "Ancient Wisdom for Modern Times" focuses on the connectivity of human experience across different eras and how it might be applied to modern times. In the framework of "The Josiah Manifesto," the teachings of the mysterious ancient monarch symbolize a reservoir of wisdom that can assist the current President of the United States of America in navigating the complexity of leadership, the issues that society faces, and the progression of the end times. The president can bring a sense of purpose, integrity, and alignment with spiritual truths to their leadership job by drawing on these ageless lessons, which will ultimately shape a more enlightened and harmonious future.

5. Navigating the End Times

In the book "The Josiah Manifesto: The Ancient Mystery & Guide for the End Times" written by Jonathan Cahn, one of the most important aspects is the concept of "Navigating the End Times." This theme most likely investigates the difficulties, responsibilities, and possibilities that individuals, such as the current President of the United States of America, encounter in eras of enormous unpredictability and prophetic significance.

- **Exploring the End Times**

Prophetic Context: According to the teachings of a variety of religions and spiritual traditions, the "end times" are typically characterized by a time of profound upheaval and metamorphosis. The voyage of the modern president of the United States of America could be framed within this perspective, in which the president's leadership corresponds with the realization of prophetic occurrences.

Preparedness on a Spiritual Level: A heightened sense of spiritual readiness is required in order to make it through the end times. It is possible that the teachings of the mysterious ancient king emphasized the significance of finding out spiritual truth, growing inner resilience, and ensuring that one's activities were aligned with a higher purpose.

Practicality and Spirituality in Balance: The difficulty for the president in the current day may be to find a balance between the practical aspects of governance and spiritual concerns. They are tasked with addressing serious societal and global concerns while simultaneously maintaining a heightened awareness of the role's greater spiritual importance.

The relevance of this to "The Josiah Manifesto" is as follows:

The exploration of ancient mysteries and how they can be applied to modern problems are both related to the book's central theme of finding one's way through the end of the world. The teachings of the mysterious ancient king could give a road map for the current president of the United States to follow in order to traverse these turbulent times with a sense of purpose, hope, and spiritual understanding.

- **Consequences & Repercussions**

Understanding the Signs: It is possible that the president will need to interpret the signs of the times and comprehend the way in which recent happenings relate to larger prophetic narratives. The teachings of the mysterious ancient ruler might offer some insights into deciphering these indicators and making judgments based on accurate information.

Promoting Righteousness and Justice: The concepts of righteousness and justice are prevalent throughout the end times. Even in the midst of chaos, these principles could serve as a compass for the leadership of the president, ensuring that his policies and actions contribute to the creation of a just and equal society.

Encouragement of Hope: The end times can be difficult to navigate, but if the president aligns himself with spiritual ideals, it could give the people hope and strengthen their resolve to persevere. They are able to instill a sense of serenity and purpose in others by acting as an example of perseverance in the face of adversities.

Conclusion: The narrative of "The Josiah Manifesto" is given a greater sense of depth and immediacy by the inclusion of the concept of "Navigating the End Times." This book investigates the connection of spirituality, government, and the relevance of history by weaving together the cryptic teachings of an ancient monarch, the present American president's leadership, and the prophetic background of the end times. The path of the president comes to represent humanity's attempt to manage unpredictable times with wisdom, honesty, and a profound connection to greater truths. The president has the ability to inspire others to embrace their roles as spiritual beings while living in a world that is undergoing dramatic change through the actions and decisions that they take.

6. Impact on the Nation

The book "The Josiah Manifesto: The Ancient Mystery and Guide for the End Times" written by Jonathan Cahn contains an essential component that focuses on the concept of "Impact on the Nation." This theme most likely examines how the deeds, decisions, and teachings of both the mysterious ancient ruler and the contemporary President of the United

States have far-reaching effects that influence the path that their respective nations take. The effect on the country could have repercussions in a variety of spheres, including the social, cultural, political, and spiritual realms.

- **Assessing the Nation's Impact**

Leadership Legacies: The mysterious ancient king and the enigmatic modern president of the United States each have the ability to leave behind a legacy that will endure for generations. Their deeds, whether founded on age-old knowledge or on the principles of current leadership, have the potential to influence the morals and goals of their nations for many generations to come.

Changes in Social Structure: The influence on the nation extends to the transformation of society. It's possible that the teachings of the mysterious old king could spark a renaissance of spiritual ideals, which will result in beneficial changes to social dynamics, interpersonal relationships, and communal cohesion.

Influence on the World: The decisions made by a modern president of the United States can have repercussions beyond the borders of the country, which can have an effect on global connections, diplomacy, and international cooperation. It is possible that their alignment with spiritual ideals will lead to a stance on the global arena that is more compassionate and cooperative.

The relevance of this to "The Josiah Manifesto" is as follows:

The concept of "Impact on the Nation" is one that emphasizes the interdependence of spirituality, history, and leadership. The teachings of the mysterious ancient king, if adopted by the current president of the United States of America, have the potential to have a transformative effect on the nation by addressing the issues it faces and directing it toward a more enlightened future.

- **Consequences & Repercussions**

Renewal on a Spiritual Level: It is possible that the teachings of the mysterious old king will spark a spiritual revival throughout the country. This regeneration may result in a collective awakening, which may then encourage individuals to reassess the importance they place on various pursuits and accept greater spiritual truths.

Equal opportunity and social justice: It is possible that measures that advance social justice, equality, and inclusivity will be driven by the president's connection with the mysterious old king's wisdom. These efforts have the potential to develop a society that is more just and peaceful.

The Reformation of Culture: The effect on the nation may result in a shift in the standards and beliefs that govern cultural practices. The country as a whole might acquire a fresh appreciation for ageless values if it adopts the practice of incorporating ancient wisdom into contemporary debate.

Conclusion: The phrase "Impact on the Nation" is the primary focus of "The Josiah Manifesto," which focuses on the crucial part that leadership, spiritual values, and historical knowledge play in determining the course of a nation's destiny. The mysterious old king's teachings, as interpreted and implemented by the current President of the United States of America, have the potential to inspire revolutionary change across a wide variety of aspects of society. In the end, this subject emphasizes the concept that personal actions, particularly those that are founded in spiritual awareness, have the capacity to influence not only the individual lives of people but also the collective trajectory of the history of a nation.

Jonathan Cahn's book "The Josiah Manifesto: The Ancient Mystery & Guide for the End Times" dives into the intriguing concept of an ordinance given in the middle of a desert 3000 years ago and its probable influence on the rise and fall of a Latin American dictator. The purpose of this conversation is to provide a critical analysis of the fundamental themes that are offered in the book by investigating the plausibility of such a scenario and the insights that it offers into the historical and sociopolitical dynamics. This analysis will be delivered in the format of a workbook, and will provide a detailed dissection of a variety of facets of the notion.

1. The Ancient Ordinance and Its Importance

An ancient ordinance that was delivered in the middle of a desert three thousand years ago is at the heart of "The Josiah Manifesto: The Ancient Mystery and Guide for the End Times," which centers on the idea that we are living in the end times. According to Jonathan Cahn, this code includes ageless principles that have the ability to influence events that occur in the present world, including the ascent to power of a Latin American tyrant and his subsequent fall from power. This section investigates the continued applicability of this ancient regulation and the possible repercussions that it may have.

The preservation of Knowledge: The premise presented by Cahn emphasizes the concept that knowledge and direction can survive regardless of location or era. Throughout the course of human history, a variety of societies have held ancient teachings, writings, and moral codes in high regard as sources of wisdom. In the event that such a regulation does in fact exist, it is possible that it contains concepts that address fundamental human needs and the issues that society faces, which would make it applicable throughout different eras.

Universality of Ethical Values: The idea of moral standards is pervasive in a variety of time periods and geographic locations. Cahn could make the case that the ancient ordinance contains concepts that mirror universal values such as compassion, equity, and justice in his argument. These principles do not belong to a particular era or part of the world; rather, they are universal principles that form the foundation of good government in any society.

Interconnectedness of Human Experience: Patterns and cycles have recurred throughout human history, such as the ascent and fall of kings, empires, and other political institutions. The idea behind Cahn's thesis is that there could be covert connections between occurrences that are at first glance unrelated. The ancient ordinance is relevant because it has the potential to uncover previously unknown links and offer insight on the factors that contributed to the occurrence of specific historical phenomena.

Lessons from Historical Figures: There is a possibility that the book will make comparisons between historical figures who followed divine guidance and modern leaders who represent comparable ideas. Figures such as King Josiah from the biblical tale are examples of people who obeyed God's commands and brought about beneficial change in the societies in which they lived. The author hopes that by evaluating these analogies, the reader would come away with an appreciation for the continued importance of supernatural guidance in leadership, especially in the present era.

Shaping the Present and Future: The significance of the ordinance resides in the alleged power of it to direct acts both in the now and in the future. It could be used as a guide for leaders to negotiate the intricacies of their responsibilities if it contains principles that promote just and equitable governance. This gives rise to the question of whether or not devotion to such values could in fact impact the course of a dictator's ascent to power and subsequent fall from power.

Changing the Way We Think About Leadership:

It's possible that reading Cahn's book will inspire readers to reevaluate their ideas towards leadership. The book questions traditional conceptions of power and authority by using an old ordinance as its guiding force as it is presented in the book. It is possible that the dynamics of governance may be reshaped, leading to leadership that is more responsible and accountable, if those in positions of authority were to base their judgments on timeless ethical ideals.

Awakening both Spiritually and Morally: A spiritual and moral reawakening might be sparked as a result of the ancient commandment, which means its applicability goes beyond politics. If what is said in the book is accurate, then it suggests that the actions and repercussions of humankind are not the only things that matter. Instead, there is a deeper spiritual dimension that can influence the way events unfold, pushing individuals and society to reflect on their behaviors and the values that guide them.

In conclusion, the idea of an ancient ordinance and its applicability, which is described in "The Josiah Manifesto," encourages readers to ruminate on the interdependence of history, spirituality, and governmental systems. Despite the fact that the concept could look mystical, its applicability can be seen in the possibility of the universality of ethical ideals, the insights that can be gained by studying historical personalities, and the concept that wisdom can survive the passage of time. In the following sections of this research, we will look into the historical analogies and socio-political processes in Latin America, with the goal of throwing light on the plausibility of the book's premise.

2. Discovering Historical Parallels: The Influence of Ancient Wisdom on Modern Leadership

Jonathan Cahn brings to light, in his book "The Josiah Manifesto: The Ancient Mystery and Guide for the End Times," the intriguing concept of an old ordinance having an influence on the rise to power and subsequent fall from power of a Latin American dictator. In order to investigate the possibility that this concept could be true, one must look into historical similarities that could shed light on the ways in which timeless principles could potentially shape modern leadership. This chapter explores historical personalities and events that are relevant to the concept of the book. It provides a glimpse into the connection between traditional knowledge and the dynamics of contemporary leadership.

Josiah: A Model of Guided Leadership: King Josiah is considered to be one of the most important individuals in the biblical story. Josiah, who reigned over the kingdom of Judah at the time of the events described in the Hebrew Bible, is said to have set out on a mission of religious reform with the goal of reestablishing righteous administration and the kingdom's devotion to divine commands. His dedication to the teachings of God served as the compass that directed his deeds. The premise of Cahn's argument might be interpreted as drawing a comparison between Josiah's leadership and the possible influence of an ancient ordinance on the leaders of today. The author of this book proposes that devotion to comparable principles could impact the behavior of leaders in the modern world, in the same way that Josiah's obedience to divine instruction brought about positive change.

Ethical Leadership in History: Throughout the course of history, there have been many leaders who have upheld ethical ideals, at times being guided by their spiritual views. For example, Mahatma Gandhi led the movement for India's independence from British rule through the use of nonviolent tactics. He was motivated by the ideals of equality and justice. The moral principles that drove Nelson Mandela's struggle against apartheid in South Africa were much more important to him than any personal ambitions he might have had. It is clear that Cahn's concept of an ancient law has a lot in common with the deeds of these historical heroes, which lends credence to the idea that leaders who are committed to moral values are able to bring about significant change.

Divine Leadership Inspiration: It is not an unheard-of notion for leaders to be guided in their decision-making by some form of supernatural inspiration. Ancient societies frequently perceived their leaders to be channeling the advice and assistance of various gods and spirits. For example, Egyptian pharaohs believed that they had been given a divine right to reign. This congruence between divine direction and the choices made by those in positions of authority is consistent with the hypothesis advanced by Cahn, according to which a long-forgotten regulation may have the power to shape the future. It compels us to question whether or not supernatural inspiration, whether actual or perceived, could in fact influence the decisions made by contemporary political leaders.

The Influence of Ethical Standards on Empires:
Ancient empires, such as the Roman Empire,
frequently adhered to particular ethical
standards or religious beliefs that influenced
government. One example of such an empire is
the Chinese Han Dynasty. The decision of the
Roman Emperor Constantine to become a
Christian had a significant impact on the
direction that the empire took and the policies
that it implemented. The author, Cahn, may
draw comparisons in his book between the
ethical ideals included in an ancient ordinance
and the influence that religious and moral
standards had on historical civilizations. This
raises questions regarding how the devotion of
a leader to such values could effect the destiny
of a nation, particularly in the context of the
dictatorships that have existed in Latin
American countries.

Dictatorship Lessons: The annals of history are
rich with examples of tyrants who abused their

power for the sake of their own personal wealth, causing enormous misery for the populations of the nations they ruled. These tyrants, ranging from Adolf Hitler to Saddam Hussein, all pursued oppressive goals while ignoring human rights and ethical issues. The thesis of the book claims that the principles of an old ordinance could combat the bad tendencies of such totalitarian leadership, perhaps reversing the course of events by fostering just and compassionate governance. This idea is presented in the form of a book.

In a nutshell, the discovery of historical analogies indicates a reoccurring theme of ethical leadership, one that is directed by ideals that are independent of both time and culture. The deeds of historical characters such as King Josiah and Mahatma Gandhi, as well as the impact that moral codes had on empires, provide clues that point to the likelihood that an ancient law could have an effect on contemporary leadership. When examining the concept of the book, it is important to take into account not only the historical analogies, which can provide valuable insights, but also the intricate sociopolitical dynamics of Latin America, as will be discussed in the next sections of this analysis.

3. Contextualizing the Impact of Ancient Wisdom on Dictatorships in Latin America

Jonathan Cahn suggests in his book "The Josiah Manifesto: The Ancient Mystery and Guide for the End Times" that an old ordinance may have played a role in the ascent to power and subsequent fall from power of a Latin American dictator. In order to determine whether or not this idea has any basis in reality, it is necessary to investigate the sociopolitical dynamics of Latin America. Historically, this region has been characterized by authoritarian governments and intricate fights for power. This part investigates the historical and cultural environment of the area in order to investigate how the principles outlined in an old ordinance might be relevant to dictatorships that have existed in Latin American countries.

Dictatorships throughout History: In the past, Latin America has seen the growth of dictatorships as a response to the region's widespread social, economic, and political unrest. In order to solidify their grip on power, tyrants across the world, from Juan Manuel de Rosas in Argentina to Fulgencio Batista in Cuba, have taken advantage of weaknesses within the cultures they rule. The premise presented by

Cahn raises the question of whether or whether the tenets of an old code could be utilized to combat the factors, such as social injustice and corruption, that can lead to the establishment of autocratic regimes.

Disparities in Socioeconomic Status: Extreme socioeconomic disparities have frequently been cited as a primary factor in the rise to power of dictators in Latin American countries. The central premise of the book is based on the idea that values that uphold justice and fairness have the capacity to reduce these inequalities and bring about more equitable society. Exploring this idea encourages us to investigate whether or not an ancient law could provide insight on economic measures that address issues of poverty and the distribution of wealth.

Instability in the Political System and Authoritarianism: Throughout the entirety of the 20th century, Latin America was buffeted by recurrent bouts of political unrest, which were frequently accompanied by periods of authoritarian leadership. Throughout the history of this region, there have been instances of leaders seizing power by military coups, which have frequently resulted in oppressive regimes. The assumption that Cahn is calling for may be understood as advocating for leadership that is anchored in principles that limit the abuse of power and curb the potential for authoritarian inclinations.

Importance of Ethical Governance in Today's World: The concept of an old law that encouraged ethical government strikes a chord with the hopes of many people living in Latin American countries who are looking for leadership that is accountable and transparent. Protests against corruption and violations of human rights have taken place across the area, with participants calling for governments that place a higher priority on the well-being of their own people. The hypothesis that Cahn proposes is consistent with these needs, which raises the potential that commitment to ethical values may impact the decisions that are made by leaders.

Taking Action in Response to Historical Trauma: In the history of Latin America, there have been occasions of state-sanctioned violence, violations of human rights, and the silencing of dissenting voices. The idea of the book may propose that the principles of an ancient ordinance could give a way to find healing and reconciliation with one another. The ability of leaders to handle historical trauma and promote unity within their societies can be enhanced through the promotion of justice and compassion.

Political paradigms are in the process of shifting: Latin America's socio-political dynamics have witnessed swings from dictatorships to democracies and vice versa on multiple occasions. The political future of the region is frequently called into doubt as a result of these shifts. In light of Cahn's premise, we are encouraged to investigate the possibility that the ideas underlying an ancient ordinance could assist political leaders in guiding their nations toward more secure and prosperous futures, irrespective of the political paradigm that is currently in place.

In conclusion, an examination of the socio-political dynamics of Latin America reveals a landscape that is ready for the research of Cahn's concept of the impact an ancient ordinance has on dictatorships. This discovery was made after the landscape was revealed by the examination of Latin America's socio-political dynamics. The concept of the book is consistent with the past experience of dictatorships in the region, as well as socioeconomic inequality, political instability, and calls for ethical government. However, the next sections of this research will go into potential obstacles and critiques that occur when attempting to ascribe the rise and fall of a dictator simply to an ancient ordinance. These sections will begin in the next section and continue through the following section.

4. Challenges and Criticisms: Examining the Ancient Ordinance Premise's Limitations

Jonathan Cahn suggests in his book "The Josiah Manifesto: The Ancient Mystery and Guide for the End Times" that an old ordinance may have played a role in the ascent to power and subsequent fall from power of a Latin American dictator. When attributing multiple complicated historical events to a single source, it is vital to closely assess the potential difficulties and objections that may arise. Although the concept offers a fascinating perspective, this evaluation must be carried out. This chapter examines a selection of these difficulties and provides an objective analysis of the premise presented throughout the book.

Complexity and Reductionism: It's possible that attributing the rise and fall of a dictator to an ancient edict alone will lead to criticism due to the reductionist nature of the explanation. The course of historical events and political dynamics is complex, and they are frequently impacted by a wide variety of factors including the state of the economy, the state of international relations, and human aspirations. The premise of Cahn's argument runs the risk of oversimplifying these intricacies since it places an emphasis on the role of a single factor.

Personal Responsibility and Free Will:
Recognizing the role that the free will and decisions of individuals had in the development of history is a significant obstacle. Even though the ideas of an ancient ordinance could provide some direction, it is ultimately up to leaders to interpret and put those principles into practice. Most of the time, personal ambitions, power battles, and strategic concerns are the things that motivate the actions of tyrants. The

concept of the book may give the impression that individual choice does not play a substantial part in determining the course of history.

Cultural and contextual variation: It's possible that some people will contend that the ideas underlying an old ordinance aren't always valid in all times and places due to differences in culture and history. Although some ethical principles may be universally applicable, their implementation may look very different depending on the cultural norms, societal institutions, and regional issues in a given area. It's possible that Cahn's hypothesis ignores the complex relationship that exists between universal truths and particular experiences.

Influence exerted by Extraneous Factors: The unfolding of political events is rarely free from the influence of other factors. The rise and fall of a dictator may be strongly influenced by actors on the international stage, economic forces, and the geopolitical dynamics of the region. It's possible that Cahn's idea doesn't sufficiently address the role that outside forces play in determining political outcomes. If these factors are ignored, the premise of the ancient ordinance might not have as much force to explain things.

The Concepts of Causality and Correlation: The difficulty lies in attempting to establish a direct causal link between the existence of the principles of an old ordinance and the occurrence of historical events. Although there is a possibility of correlations, causality cannot be demonstrated without strong empirical proof. It's possible that reviewers will contend that the concept of the book is not supported by empirical evidence and instead leans heavily on speculative interpretation.

Various Historical Pathways: The histories of dictatorships in Latin America have taken many different paths, each of which has been shaped by a unique combination of historical, cultural, and social elements. If one were to try to trace these differences merely to the influence of an ancient law, one may miss the region's distinctive historical experiences and the complexities that come along with them.

In conclusion, despite the fact that the idea of an old ordinance having an effect on historical events is intriguing, there are considerable obstacles and potential critiques that may be leveled against it. The simplifying of complex events, underestimating the agency of individuals, and overlooking the influence of outside variables are all examples of these issues. In order to provide a valid analysis, one must first evaluate the premise of the book in a fair and objective manner, while also taking into account the complex and multidimensional nature of historical trajectories. In the following parts of this examination, we are going to look deeper into the wider spiritual and philosophical implications of the idea, as well as its importance for the end times.

5. Exploring the Nexus of Divine Guidance and Human Agency

Jonathan Cahn explores the startling possibility, presented in his book "The Josiah Manifesto: The Ancient Mystery and Guide for the End Times," that an old ordinance could have a role in the ascent to power or fall from power of a

Latin American dictator. This idea digs quite far into the fields of spirituality and philosophy, examining the complex dynamic that exists between heavenly direction and free will in individuals. This chapter explores the broader ramifications of the book's thesis by looking at the spiritual and philosophical facets that are encompassed by it.

Divine Intervention and Human Free Will: The ideas presented by Cahn provoke deep consideration regarding the appropriate relationship between divine intervention and the free will of individuals. If a long-forgotten law has the power to affect historical developments, this points to the existence of some degree of deterministic influence. This raises the question of whether or not human decisions are directed by a divine plan, or whether or not individuals retain the ability to make decisions that have an impact on their own destinies.

Moral Accountability and Governance: The premise of the book emphasizes the importance of moral accountability for leaders. If a precedence ordinance from a bygone era includes guidelines for moral administration, then it follows that those in positions of authority have a duty to ensure that these guidelines are followed for the benefit of society as a whole. This gives rise to philosophical discussions regarding the ethical responsibilities of leaders and the repercussions of disregarding these fundamental principles.

Determinism and Historical Patterns: Cahn's theory has a deterministic component, with the implication that historical patterns may have been determined by the guidance of heavenly intelligence. This gives rise to the question of whether or not events take place in accordance with a predetermined plan, or whether or not there is room for chance and unpredictability in the course of human history. Investigating these consequences requires delving into philosophical discussions that have been going on for a long time about determinism and fate.

Ethical Foundations of Leadership: The premise encourages contemplation of the underlying ideas that ought to serve as a compass for the decisions that are made by leaders. If an old ordinance gives ageless knowledge for equitable and compassionate administration, then it presents a challenge for leaders to review their actions in light of these principles and make adjustments as necessary. This investigation gives rise to conversations regarding the ethical underpinnings of leadership and the repercussions of straying from those underpinnings.

Intersection of Spirituality and Politics: The concept of the book brings together two fields that, at first glance, couldn't be more different: spirituality and politics. It implies that political happenings and the decisions that politicians make might be influenced by supernatural guidance. This intersection provokes thought about the more general role that spirituality plays in the formation of society structures and governance, as well as the question of whether or not spiritual principles may direct policies and behaviors.

Unity and Common Purpose: Individuals have a better chance of coming together to work toward a similar goal if the concepts that underlie an old regulation can be applied in a variety of contexts. Regardless of the cultural or historical gaps that exist, the concept of sticking to eternal ethical standards has the potential to encourage cooperation. This idea sparks philosophical debates concerning the all-pervasive nature of moral values and the part they play in the process of bringing people together as a society.

In conclusion, the consequences of the book's thesis in terms of spirituality and philosophy go beyond the scope of historical analysis. Consideration should be given to the connection between divine guidance and human agency, the ethical responsibilities of those in positions of authority, and the interdependence of spiritual values and political systems as a result of this idea. Whether or not one subscribes to the concept, it acts as a stimulus for significant talks concerning the complicated interplay between spiritual beliefs, philosophical perspectives, and the course of historical events. This is true regardless of whether or not one subscribes to the concept. In the following sections of this examination, we will investigate the concept's applicability in the context of the end times and the ways in which it has the capacity to direct leadership in the modern era.

6. The End-Times Relevance: Navigating Uncertainty Through Ancient Wisdom

In his book "The Josiah Manifesto: The Ancient Mystery & Guide for the End Times," Jonathan Cahn discusses the possibility of an old ordinance having an influence on the rise to power and subsequent fall from power of a Latin American dictator. A relationship between this idea and the biblical concept of the "End Times" is suggested by the fact that the book is titled "End Times." This section investigates the importance of the notion within the framework of eschatology and investigates the ways in which ancient knowledge may assist individuals and societies in navigating times of uncertainty and transition.

Prophecy and Divine Guidance: The phrase "End Times" is frequently linked to the interpretation of prophesies and the involvement of the divine. The notion that Cahn is proposing is consistent with the belief that ancient wisdom, communicated in the form of an ordinance, has the potential to provide direction amid turbulent times that some people consider to be the "End Times." In light of this, the notion of divine intervention in molding historical events and the choices made by leaders is brought into question at a time when the globe is navigating through moments of great uncertainty.

The Deterioration of Ethical Foundations:
Eschatological ideas frequently place an emphasis on moral and ethical grounds in light of the extraordinary problems that mankind is currently facing. The idea of an ancient law gives the impression that these moral precepts can survive the test of time and continue to serve as a reliable guidance even when conventional institutions become unstable. The premise of the book is consistent with the thought that maintaining adherence to one's

ethical beliefs becomes even more important when facing unpredictability.

Spiritual Awakening and Transformation: The concepts of spiritual reawakening and metamorphosis are frequently included in eschatological belief systems. The idea that divine guidance can cause substantial alterations in both an individual's and a community's state of awareness is congruent with Cahn's description of an ancient ordinance. It is possible that the spiritual transformation that is required to successfully traverse the intricacies of the "End Times" will be made easier if leaders and civilizations pay attention to these ideas.

Addressing Challenges on a Global Scale: The phrase "End Times" is commonly used to refer to difficult times on a worldwide scale, including times of war, natural disasters, and societal upheaval. The thesis of the book is that it offers answers to solve these difficulties through ethical governance. This interpretation is open to interpretation. It begs the question of whether or not sticking to eternal principles can help alleviate the worldwide crises that are typically connected with eschatological narratives.

Human Nature in Reflection: Eschatological talks usually center on the inherent failings of humanity as well as the opportunity for human beings to be redeemed. The idea of an ancient law may stimulate introspection into human nature, the decisions that individuals make, and the effects those decisions have on civilizations. As people get ready for the unpredictability of the future, it highlights how important it is for them to do ethical self-reflection.

Implications for Leadership and Governance: Leadership assumes an even greater significance when viewed in the perspective of the so-called "End Times." It is possible that leaders of civilizations that are going through turbulent times are those that base their decisions on the ideals contained inside an ancient code. This raises concerns about the role of leaders in times of uncertainty and if divine knowledge can give a model for responsible and ethical administration. Additionally, this raises problems about the role of leaders in times of uncertainty.

To summarize, the concept of an ancient ordinance's influence on historical events acquires additional significance when viewed within the context of the "End Times." It does this by connecting eschatological concepts like as divine guidance, ethical underpinnings, and spiritual development with the dynamics of historical events. Regardless of whether one chooses to take these concepts literally or interpret them figuratively, they provoke thought-provoking conversations on the interplay of spirituality, history, and the unpredictability of the future. In the following sections of this analysis, we will investigate the potential impact that an ancient ordinance could have on contemporary leadership, as well as the consequences that this could have for the formation of a society that is just and compassionate.

Conclusion

Jonathan Cahn spins a story that spans both time and cultures in his book "The Josiah Manifesto: The Ancient Mystery and Guide for the End Times." This story suggests that an old ordinance may have played a role in the rise and fall of a Latin American dictator. Cahn's book is titled "The Ancient Mystery and Guide for the End Times." This analysis has examined the different components of the concept through the lens of a multifaceted investigation. Additionally, it has contextualized the notion within historical parallels and sociopolitical dynamics, and it has dug into the spiritual and philosophical ramifications of the concept.

The idea that an old law could have had an impact on what happened in the past piques our interest and provokes thought and discussion. Despite the fact that the idea presents an intriguing viewpoint, it is necessary to approach it in a critical manner. The investigation brought to light a number of difficulties, including the simplifying of intricate historical occurrences, the significance of individual agency, and the impact of external circumstances. These difficulties call for a sophisticated evaluation of the extent to which an ancient statute can directly influence the path that dictatorships take.

The story told in this book is resonant with historical analogies, which serve to show the lasting nature of ethical leadership, divine guidance, and the quest of justice by humans. The complexity of Latin American dictatorships, on the other hand, is not simply defined by an old ordinance. It is necessary to conduct an in-depth investigation into the socioeconomic gaps, political battles, and external forces that shape these regimes.

In addition, the spiritual and philosophical aspects that were investigated shed light on the complex link that exists between human action and the knowledge of a higher power. This idea provokes thought on topics such as determinism, ethical governance, and the intersection between spirituality and politics. Regardless of where one stands with regard to the concept's believability, it provokes conversation about the place of spirituality in political leadership and the quest for justice in society.

The fact that this idea is connected to the so-called "End Times" increases its overall relevance and gives it eschatological overtones. The book claims that guidance from the past might help mankind navigate through uncertain futures by interweaving ancient wisdom with prophetic narratives. This idea is presented in the context of the book. The concept's relevance within broader discussions about humanity's purpose and direction is amplified as a result of this blend of historical contemplation, spiritual understanding, and prophetic vision.

A tapestry constructed from historical echoes, spiritual echoes, and philosophical reflections, "The Josiah Manifesto: The Ancient Mystery & Guide for the End Times" is an apt summary of this work. The investigation that was carried out in this research sheds light on the various layers of the notion, ranging from the historical similarities to the eschatological importance. It places an emphasis on the need for a holistic perspective that recognizes the multifaceted character of history, human agency, and the potential for ancient wisdom to guide contemporary cultures toward justice, compassion, and ethical leadership. Specifically, it highlights the need for a holistic perspective that acknowledges the multidimensional nature of history. Regardless of whether the idea finally rings true as an everlasting reality or as a metaphor for the imagination, there is no denying that it has opened doors to introspection and conversation regarding the interaction between heavenly guidance and human activities.

Jonathan Cahn's "The Josiah Manifesto: The Ancient Mystery & Guide for the End Times" is a thought-provoking book that digs into America's and the world's prospective paths as they negotiate the difficulties of modern times. This workbook analysis will look at the book's core themes and concepts, as well as its ramifications for the future and the concept of calamity. We will evaluate the book's key principles, examine its perspective on America's fate, consider its views about the world's future, and remark on its overall relevance by following a planned pattern.

1. Fundamental Ideas

Cahn's work uses historical and biblical perspectives to illuminate current and future occurrences. The book's central theme is the importance of recognizing and responding to heavenly warnings, as shown by the narrative of King Josiah in ancient times. Cahn's presentation of the Josiah Manifesto is a call to learn from history and connect one's actions with spiritual truths.

2. The Potential Trajectory of America in "The Josiah Manifesto"

In the book "The Josiah Manifesto:

Jonathan Cahn, explores the probable destiny of America based on historical and spiritual truths. Cahn offers a thought-provoking take on the nation's fate by drawing parallels between ancient Israel's decline and current America's issues. Let's look at how the book sees America's future and its possible link to disaster:

Historical Comparisons: Cahn contends that America's path parallels the historical trajectory of ancient Israel. He draws parallels between moral and spiritual deterioration in both countries, emphasizing how contempt for ethical standards and spiritual principles can lead to societal upheaval and disaster.

Divine Forewarnings: The theme of divine warnings—signals from a higher power alerting nations to their mistakes—is emphasized throughout the book. Cahn claims that, like ancient Israel, America has had its fair share of warnings in the form of numerous events, crises, and even natural disasters. These occurrences are understood as summons to introspection and transformation.

Moral and ethical deterioration: Cahn covers current topics including moral relativism, ethical decay, and the disintegration of traditional values. He contends that these elements contribute to societal decline, eerily similar to the tendencies observed in ancient Israel prior to its demise.

Repentance on a National Scale: The story urges national remorse and spiritual rebirth. Cahn advises that America's leaders and population reassess their beliefs and realign with higher principles, just as King Josiah led ancient Israel in returning to God's ways. This, he claims, has the ability to change the country's trajectory.

Aversion to Catastrophe: While the book does not overtly forecast disaster, it emphasizes the importance of course adjustment in order to avoid possible disasters. Cahn's message is one of urgency: address the underlying causes of society decay and work actively toward spiritual and moral rebirth.

Individual and Group Responsibility: Cahn emphasizes both individual and collective accountability. He claims that every citizen plays a part in molding the nation's future, emphasizing the ability of personal transformation to impact the larger socioeconomic environment.

Hope and Recovery: Despite the fact that the book discusses potential disasters, it also contains a message of optimism. Cahn depicts the possibility of national rebirth and restoration if citizens and leaders embrace spiritual ideals and make ethical decisions.

Action Is Needed: Finally, America's direction in "The Josiah Manifesto" serves as a call to action. Readers are urged to reflect on their own lives, engage in self-reflection, and actively contribute to constructive social change. Individuals can help shape a more aligned and robust future for the country by identifying historical trends and divine warnings.

In conclusion, "The Josiah Manifesto" portrays America's prospective trajectory as being dependent on the country's reaction to moral and spiritual difficulties. The book pushes for national introspection, repentance, and a return to ethical norms by establishing parallels with past history and imploring citizens to heed divine warnings. While acknowledging potential disasters, the book highlights the possibility of constructive transformation and restoration via individual and societal actions.

3. The Future of the World

Cahn's thoughts go beyond the United States, addressing global challenges and potential disasters. He emphasizes the interconnection of nations and how international events can affect the entire world. While not a doomsday prediction, the book emphasizes the importance of individuals and nations reevaluating their ideals in order to promote a more harmonious and sustainable future. Cahn's method invites readers to consider the broader ramifications of their actions and decisions.

4. Workbook Pattern Analysis

Theme Introduction: Begin by explaining the book's primary topics, focusing on how it uses historical and spiritual backgrounds to explore current and future difficulties.

America's Destiny: Make a section about Cahn's thoughts on America's impending disaster. Compare and contrast historical Israel with modern America, highlighting the importance of moral and ethical decisions in defining a nation's destiny.

From a Global Perspective: Transition to addressing the book's predictions for the future of the globe. Consider the interconnection of nations, worldwide events, and the importance of global collaboration and understanding.

The Manifesto of Josiah: Explore the concept of The Josiah Manifesto itself, which is a plea to heed warnings, learn from history, and connect with spiritual truths. Consider the ramifications for personal development and society change.

Practical Insights: Present the book's practical implications, such as the value of self-awareness, ethical decision-making, and the pursuit of spiritual ideals. Encourage readers to consider their own roles in creating the future.

Importance and Criticism: Consider the importance of Cahn's book in the perspective of current debates about spirituality, ethics, and society growth. Address any potential objections of the technique or ideas in the book.

Summarize: Summarize the main points raised throughout the workbook analysis. Individual and collectively, emphasize the importance of identifying warning signals, making informed decisions, and striving toward a more positive future.

Conclusion: Jonathan Cahn's "The Josiah Manifesto" offers a distinct view on America's and the world's prospective directions, combining historical and spiritual ideas as a guiding framework. Using a structured workbook style, this analysis has investigated the book's fundamental principles, perspectives on America's fate and the future of the globe, and overall significance. The book invites readers to take an active role in crafting a better future by studying history, identifying warning signals, and aligning with higher principles.

Cahn's observations serve as a call to action for individuals and nations alike as we traverse the difficulties of the modern world.

Jonathan Cahn's The Josiah Manifesto: The Ancient Mystery & Guide for the End Times is a thought-provoking and spiritually illuminating book that explores the ageless themes of history, prophecy, and religion. Cahn effectively weaves old biblical events with contemporary societal difficulties in this book, providing readers with a unique perspective on the challenges and opportunities given by the modern world. Cahn asks readers to ponder on the significance of the past, the urgency of the present, and the hope of the future through a painstaking investigation of historical and prophetic similarities.

The story revolves around King Josiah, a historical and biblical figure noted for his vital role in rehabilitating Judah amid a period of moral decay and spiritual collapse. Cahn finds startling connections between Josiah's situation and the issues confronting today's society. He claims that, just as Josiah's acts resulted in a spiritual awakening and a return to God, a similar transformation is required today to traverse the intricacies of the modern world.

Cahn's engaging narrative style draws readers in and encourages them to evaluate the significance of ancient knowledge in today's society. Cahn elucidates the possible impact of individual and collective actions on the course of nations by exploring the historical significance of Josiah's reign. He advocates for a return to fundamental values, highlighting the significance of seeking spiritual guidance in an age of ambiguity and moral relativism.

Cahn skilfully navigates a maze of biblical prophecies throughout the book, revealing links between ancient predictions and modern happenings. He emphasizes how the hardships and conflicts of the end times were predicted in the scriptures, providing readers with a road map for understanding the world's chaotic state. In doing so, he not only informs but also inspires readers to participate in self-reflection and discernment, developing a stronger connection to their faith and purpose.

The Josiah Manifesto is a call to action as much as a book of eschatological analysis. Cahn challenges readers to analyze their lives, make real choices, and become agents of good transformation in a world that can feel overwhelming at times. He emphasizes the significance of accepting personal responsibility for one's views, behaviors, and societal contributions. This book's motivational feature allows readers to actively shape the direction of their lives and the world around them.

To summarize, Jonathan Cahn's The Josiah Manifesto: The Ancient Mystery & Guide for the End Times is a captivating study that bridges the gap between ancient knowledge and current concerns. Cahn's deft storytelling, profound insights, and nuanced links between history, prophecy, and faith combine to form a thorough guide to navigating the intricacies of the modern era. Cahn asks us to go on a journey of spiritual renewal and transformation by urging readers to reflect on their beliefs, align their behaviors with their ideals, and accept their role as catalysts for positive change. This book serves as a timely reminder that, regardless of the uncertainties of the times, a firm commitment to faith, righteousness, and the search of truth can illuminate the route forward.

Made in the USA
Las Vegas, NV
29 October 2023

79901574R00075